The Importance of Drinking Water, with Grandpa Fisher

Copyright © 2020 by Nikki T. Fisher

Illustrated by Jasmine T. Mills
Edited by Elaine Shelly

Published in Jonesboro, Georgia, by Nikki T. Fisher

All rights reserved. No part of this book may be reproduced, stored in a retrieval system, transmitted by any means, mechanical or electronic, photocopying, recording or otherwise without the written permission of the publisher.

ISBN: 978-1-7353162-0-8

Contact: nikki@imaginnewellness.com
Printed in the United States of America

Subscribe to my email mail list on my website www.Imaginnewellness.com

This Book Belongs to:

_____

Date: _____

This book is dedicated to the legacy of my Grandpa Floyd G. Fisher, Sr. My grandpa taught me so many valuable life lessons. I did not understand then, but those now-understood lessons are the reasons for writing this book in his honor.
-Dr. Nikki Fisher

This book is about the lesson my grandpa taught me about the importance of drinking water.

"Nikki! Did you drink your water today?"

Grandpa Fisher loved his granddaughter and knew he had to remind her to take care of herself.

Nikki was used to his daily reminders but scrunched her face at this reminder.

"No! Grandpa, I do not like water. It tastes nasty and has no flavor."

"Have a glass of water with me, Nikki!"

They both went to the kitchen. Grandpa Fisher poured them a glass of water and tried to gently convince her to drink. He added, "Can you grab the watermelon from the fridge?"

Nikki removed the watermelon from the refrigerator. She repeated, "I tried to drink water before. I can't, I just can't do it."

She thought about his reminder for a moment. She knew he only wanted the best for her.

She asked, "Grandpa, can you tell me again why drinking water is so important?"

Grandpa smiled at Nikki. He liked it when she asked him questions. She would remember his lessons when she asked questions. "Yes, of course I will, dear. Have a seat and let us chat, so I can tell you again about the importance of water."

He pointed to the living room and Nikki followed him. He placed the water jug and the bowl of watermelon on the coffee table.

Nikki understood what her grandfather said but was disappointed. "Grandpa, I really wish I liked drinking water. I wish I could drink it cause now I know my body needs it."

After they sat down, he continued, "Water is an essential nutrient. We must drink it in order to stay healthy and vibrant. We cannot live without water. Our body is made of 70% water."

Grandpa was not discouraged by Nikki's dislike of water.

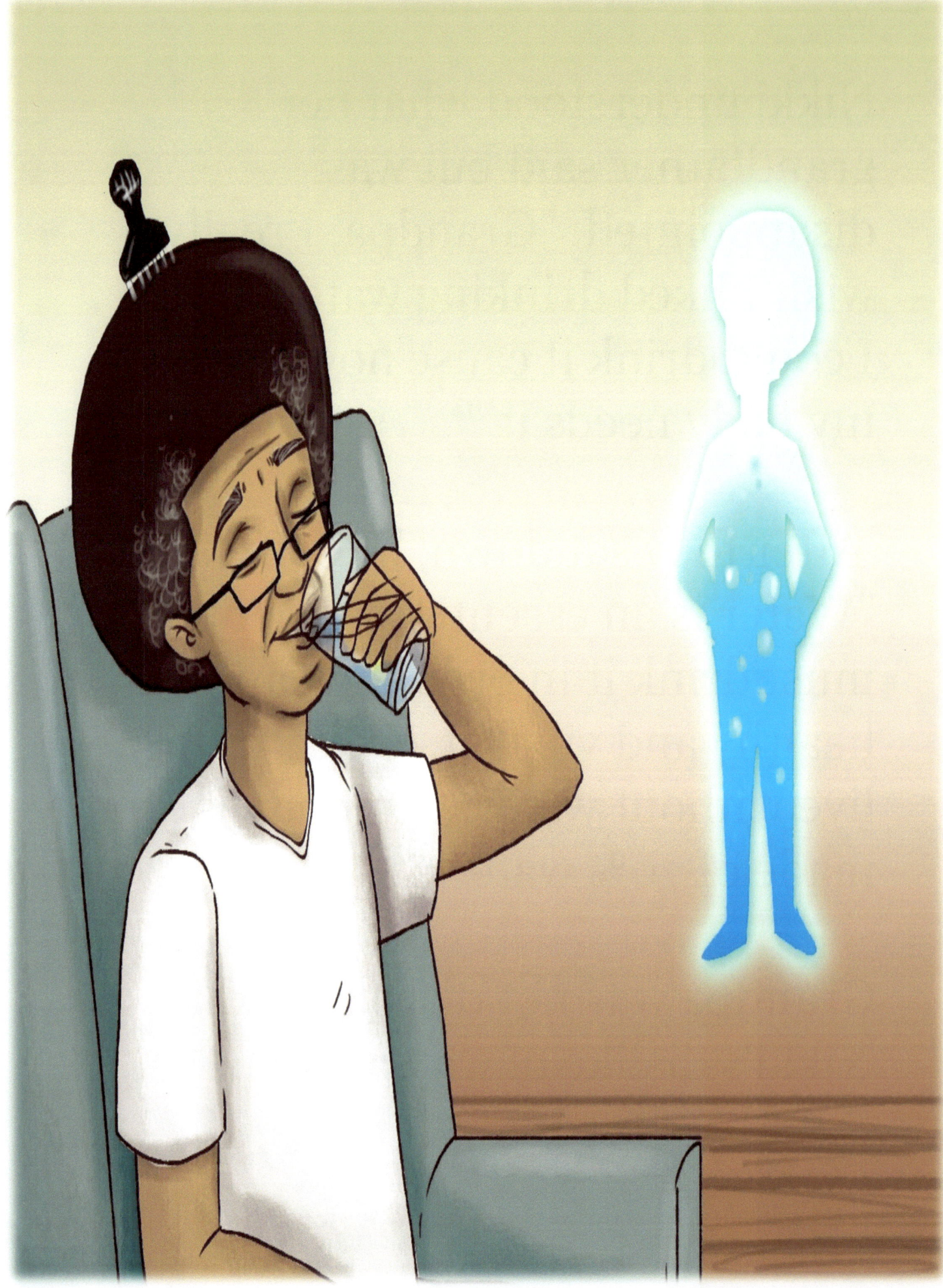

He continued to explain, "Water is needed by our organs for hydration and proper function. Our organs cannot work well without enough water." Nikki listened closely to her grandpa. She was amazed at how much he knew about water.

"Grandpa, that is some good information."

"Water provides us with oxygen," he said as he continued his lesson on water.

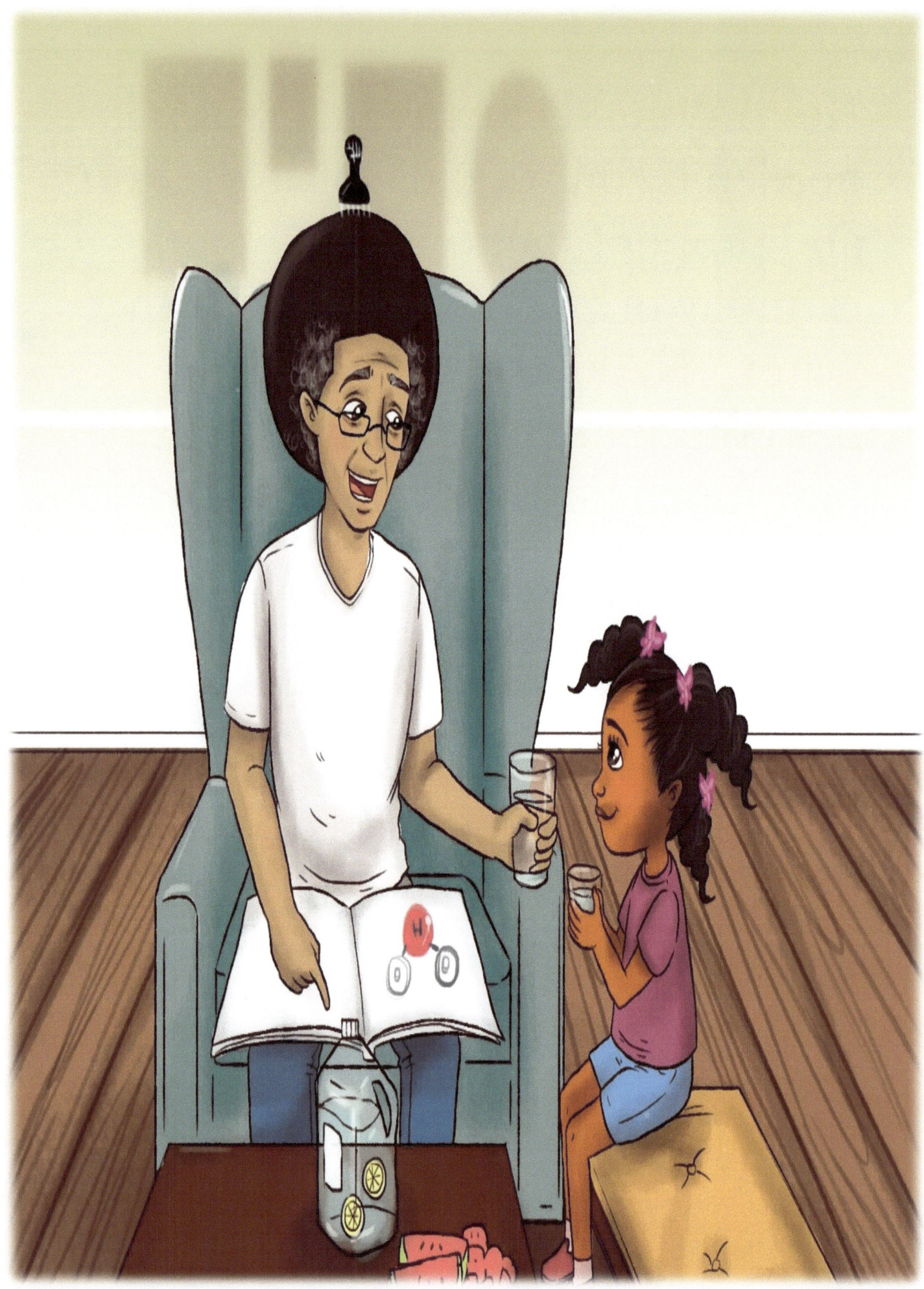

"Water is made up of a molecule that has 2 hydrogen atoms and 1 oxygen atom. We call a molecule of water, H_2O."

As Nikki listened, she felt smarter. She repeated it to herself so she wouldn't forget – "H_2O, WOW! grandpa, you are very smart for knowing all about water.

"Water is designed to break up chemical bonds," he waved his hands to show her chemical bonds breaking. "Water has the power to detoxify your organs, especially your liver."

Grandpa pointed to her stomach to show where her liver is. "Detoxify means to remove waste or things that could possibly harm us and make us ill. Waste is the stuff inside your body that our bodies don't need, use or want." Grandpa smiled at Nikki again. He knew she understood his lesson on water.

"Ooh Grandpa, please give me some more H_2O. From now on I am going to call water H_2O."

Grandpa filled her glass with water. She took a big gulp of water. Nikki tasted water and lemons. It was good.

"Okay Grandpa, from this day forward, I am going to drink all the H_2O I can, "Nikki promised. "I now know that H_2O is an essential nutrient for our organs and body. H_2O helps our bodies to naturally detox and that means get rid of stuff our bodies do not need or could possibly harm us."

Grandpa smiled as he kissed Nikki's forehead.

"Nikki, you have made your grandpa proud."

Nikki got an idea as she looked at the bowl of watermelon. "Grandpa, even though I do not like drinking H_2O, I understand why it's important to drink. To make sure I drink more H_2O, I am going to put watermelon in my glass of H_2O to give it flavor. Then it won't taste so nasty."

Grandpa was delighted by Nikki's idea. He watched her take a big gulp of water and wanted to celebrate. "Nikki, that is a great idea. I am proud of you for drinking your water. Let us toast to that."

Nikki raised her almost-empty glass of water to a toast.

"Grandpa, I like drinking my H_2O with lemons and yummy-tasting watermelon. It tastes good! I am so glad you are my grandpa. You are so smart and teach me great lessons. I love you, Grandpa."

Grandpa smiled at her and said, "I love you, too, dear."

THE END

This is a picture of my Grandpa Fisher and me.

ABOUT THE AUTHOR
DR. NIKKI T. FISHER

Since the passing of her Grandpa Fisher on April 10, 2003. Dr. Fisher has dedicated her life to health, wellness and fitness. Grandpa Fisher was such an inspiration to not only her life but the lives of many others. He contributed to the discovery of her passion for health, wellness and fitness. She is a natural-born entrepreneur, which he was too. She attributes that gift to her Grandpa Fisher as well. Nikki opened her first business in 2003, the year her Grandpa passed. She started her second business, Imaginne Wellness, in his honor. The name of second business was GOD-inspired. The second business includes health coaching, nutrition, holistic health, wellness, fitness, massage therapy and soon chiropractic practice. Dr. Fisher is currently a student attending Life University Chiropractic Doctorate Program in Marietta, GA. By 2022, she will finish her studies and become a Doctor of Chiropractic, a holistic doctor. She also plans to become a Health club franchisee soon. Soon after her grandpa passed in 2003, she obtained a naturopathic certification and became a Naturopathic Doctor. All this has led her to write children's books about the lessons that have inspired her.

Thank you for reading this book

CONTACT INFORMATION

www.Imaginnewellness.com
Nikki@imaginnewellness.com
IG: www.instagram.com/imaginnewellness
FB: www.facebook.com/imaginnewellness
YouTube: Imaginne Wellness

Subscribe to my email mail list on my website

www.ingramcontent.com/pod-product-compliance
Lightning Source LLC
Chambersburg PA
CBHW060810090426
42736CB00003B/218